Rothenburg on the Tauber

© 1978, Edm. von König-Verlag, D - 6909 Dielheim, Federal Republic of Germany, Postfach 1027
Photographs: Willy Sauer, Dielheim (except the
inside of St. Jacob's Church: Fa. A. Ohmayer,
Rothenburg; p. 47: Ingeborg Limmer, Bamberg;
p. 69: aerial photograph Fa. Elsässer, permitted
by the Reg. Präs. 9/10 253; p. 82/83: aerial
photograph Carl Zeiss, Oberkochen, permitted by
the Reg. Präs. Nordw. 031/00423)
Text: Wolfgang Kootz, Heidelberg
English Translation: Thomas Wendling, Heidelberg
Set up: Hellmuth Roth, CH - Herrliberg
Setting: Chemigraphisches Institut AG, CH - Glatt-
brugg
Photolithos and print: Vontobel-Druck AG,
CH - Feldmeilen
Cover: Benziger AG, CH - Einsiedeln
ISBN: 3-921 934-00-1

Willi Sauer/Wolfgang Kootz

Rothenburg
on the Tauber

Edm. von König-Verlag, Heidelberg

Contents

Silhouette of the medieval town with the vaulted bridge over the Taubergrund.

Rothenburg on the Tauber (Rothenburg ob der Tauber)

This formerly independent imperial town is a meeting place of countless tourists from all over the world. Their numbers compare only with the visitors to Munich, Berlin, Hamburg, and the citadels and castles along the Rhine, in upper Bavaria or in Heidelberg. Rothenburg is supposedly the most complete preserved medieval town. Elevated above neighbouring Dinkelsbühl, Nördlingen and Schwäbisch Hall, picturesque Rothenburg is situated on a plateau at the edge of a steep incline formed by the Tauber River as it washed out its bed 60 m (200 ft) below. Consequently the surname "ob (above) der Tauber" is justified. As one approaches the town from the west side, roofs and towers of various shapes and sizes elevate over the green hill and the line of the town wall to form a wonderfully lively silhouette. Hence, a walk through the Tauber Valley and up onto the top of the Engelsburg (engel castle) can create the most memorable impression of a Rothenburg visit.

The Earls of Rothenburg

The first indications of settlement in this area are the remains of the ring wall from the Engelsburg built by the Kelts as a Fliehburg (refuge castle) against the advancing Teutons/Germans. The settlement itself had its origin on the ledge which follows along the Tauber River. This already strategically convenient site was further strengthened during the fifth century by a crude tower apparently erected by the Franconian Duke Pharamund. This so-called Pharamund Tower stood in the present Burggarten (castle gardens) until 1802 when it was then torn down. Shortly before the change of the millennium, the Earls of Rothenburg appear in the light of history. In 962, Earl Reinger erected the parsonage Detwang in the Tauber Valley and the castle on the mountain projection. As well Reinger who at the same time was Earl of Maulachgau and Kochergau bought the Kahen Mountain near Schwäbisch Hall from the Bishop of Augsburg Luitpold in 990, and there erected the castle Komburg. At first his royal lineage was called "von Rothenburg" (of Rothenburg) and later "von Komberg" (of Komberg) and became the most powerful family in Ostfranken (East Franconia). The heraldic figure, a lion's head with two rafters in its mouth, can be found at different locations in Rothenburg and at the Komburg. The Komburg became the residence for the Earls of Kochergau while the Maulachgau region was administered from Rothenburg. Burkhard of Komburg changed the Komburg into a monastery in 1075 and 1081. His brother Heinrich had also remained childless, and willed his possessions to the Komburg monastery when he died in 1116. With him the bloodlines of the Earls of Rothenburg-Komburg as well died out. The name Rothenburg has no apparent connection with the colour "rot" (red) since the oldest castle was built out of grey shell lime. Historians attribute the first part of the word to the German verb "roden" (to cultivate) or to an Earl Ruodo (Rüdiger).

The Rothenburg in the possession of the Hohenstaufen

According to the will of Earl Heinrich, Emperor Heinrich lent the "ostfränkische" districts to his nephew Duke Konrad von Schwaben (of Swabia), and hence this Rothenburg came into possession of the Hohenstaufen. In 1137 Konrad became king of the German empire. In front of the Earl's castle called the Hinterburg (back castle), he built the Reichsfeste (empire fortress) or the Kaiserburg (emperor's castle) and resided in Rothenburg. At Konrad's death his son was just eight years old, and therefore Konrad's nephew Friedrich I Barbarossa was elected king. In 1157 Friedrich, the so-called child of Rothenburg, was knighted at thirteen years of age. His cousin Barbarossa later nominated him Duke of Rothenburg and granted Swabia and Ostfranken to him, but kept the original country of the Earls of Rothenburg. Since one's residence was accorded by rank, the castle became a great attraction of the chivalrous life. During this time, Rothenburg was highly valued since the plateau offered natural protection, and consequently a settlement of craftsmen, tradespeople and noblemen blossomed. Already in 1167, the hand of fate followed. The current twenty-two year old Duke Friedrich nicknamed "der Schöne" (the nice) had accompanied his cousin Friedrich Barbarossa on a military expedition to Italy. Here an epidemic was raging, and took the life of the young duke. His remains rest in the church of the Ebrach Monastery in lower Franconia. The inheritance was gained by the Emperor Friedrich Barbarossa who administered the Franconian properties of Rothenburg through Truchsesse.

The Claim of the Town

In 1172 Emperor Friedrich Barbarossa granted town rights to the now enlarged settlement. Consequently, it was allowed to hold a market once weekly, and the simple fences and stockades were replaced by ramparts strengthened by towers. In the west and south, the townwalls followed the upper edge of the Tauber Valley, half-encircling today's Johannis Church and onto the former Dominican Nunnery. This completed the oldest defence circuit which can easily be followed by the rows of houses. At the Alten Keller (old cave) for example, a simple gate flanked by the mighty Marcus Tower belonged to the oldest town fortification along with the Weisse Turm (white tower). Altogether this town fortification stretched 1400 m (around 1530 yds).

First Extension of the Town Rampart

Although barely completed, the rampart circuit was already too narrow. The population had increased significantly, and additional space for dwellings and monasteries was needed. Hence, the town around 1204 began to construct a new defence rampart whose shape approximated today's remains. The Spitalviertel (former hospital district) situated south of the enclosing Siebers Tower became protected in the fourteenth century. This new course of the rampart extended the fortification line to 2400 m (around 2625 yd). The Kobolzeller Gate, the Siebers Tower, the Röder Gate, the Würzburger Gate, and the Klingen Gate now formed the fortified town gates while smaller towers supported the rampart. From the original fortification circuit, there remained only the outlines with the Castle Gate at the border of the valley. The existing lanes which lead to the rampart were simply extended. The old town rampart including the newly aquired ground was sold piece by piece to construction-willing citizens. During this time, four monasteries had settled between the walls: the Johanniters, the Deutschherrens, the Dominicans, and the Franciscans. The Deutschherrens especially held important political rights. When in 1251, the town was mortgaged from the Emperor to Gottfried von Hohenlohe, the town itself was able to settle the debt. In 1274 Rothenburg was granted the status of an independent imperial town by the new Emperor Rudolf von Habsburg. Consequently it was placed under the command of the emperor himself, and gained its own administration and jurisdiction.

The fountain at the western section of the town hall's double structure was layed in 1250. It has remained with its high tower until today.

The Kappenzipfel

During these hostile times, many persons living outside of the fortification streamed into the protected town. In particular many slaves gained their freedom since they were not reclaimed by their masters within the stipulated one year. As a result of population expansion and land shortage, important facilities such as the Hospital zum Heiligen Geist (to the Holy Ghost) became situated outside of the town rampart. Hence, the Rothenburgers required an extension of their town fortification towards the south. Initially Emperor Albrecht I was reluctant to permit the expansion, but allegedly said that the ground plan would look like a jelly bag anyways, so it may as well have its tip. That gave the new town district the nickname "Kappenzipfel" (tip of the cap). After this delay, the wall was again extended for 1000 m (around 1094 yd) to 3400 m (around 3718 yd). In 1324 and 1349 Rothenburg was mortgaged by the emperor. If the town had enough wealth, it could itself buy freedom during this time. From the year 1339 the town was allowed to form alliances, and in 1352 it acquired independence from the empire and gained blood jurisdiction. The entire fortification was destroyed by an earthquake in 1356. From the impressive Staufer Fort there remained only the "hohe Haus der Herzöge" later called the Blasius Chapel. In the middle of the fourteenth century, the double bridge was erected, and by 1373 construction had begun on St. Jacob's Church which replaced the old parish church.

Bürgermeister Toppler

At the end of the fourteenth century, the power of the emperors had declined, the knights had become poor, and in their importance the towns had approached the sovereigns. Rothenburg at this time joined the Swabian town alliance.

Heinrich Toppler originated from a rich family, and together with his wife donated the high altar in the St. Jacob's Church (1388). A remaining certificate explains: "In 1373 the nobles and the town's people in Franconia were in great discord. The nobles had even wished to destroy the town, and hence the town was angry with these nobles, the sovereigns, and the masters. Heinrich Toppler from Rothenburg uff der Tauber was the captain of Ulm, Nördlingen, Dinkelsbühl, and several other towns. They even travelled to the Rhine in pursuit of their enemies." Toppler, Bürgermeister and army leader at the same time, drew such respect that even the controversial King Wenzel (1378–1400) often visited the Topplerschlösschen (Toppler castle). This strange residence was erected for Toppler in the Tauber Valley in the Romanique noble style. Out of the fortification remains he built the Blasius Chapel and used the mineral spring in the valley for a bath called Wildbath. After Wenzel was voted out of power in 1400, a plot against Toppler was instigated by the Burggraf Friedrich of Nürnberg. This ended with the destruction of the surrounding cultivated country controlled by Rothenburg and with an unfavourable conclusion of peace in 1408. In the same year, letters of Toppler sent to the former King Wenzel came into the hands of King Ruprecht of Palatinia. The Bürgermeister was subsequently thrown into the town-hall dungeon for suspicion of conspiracy. There he died three months later. However, the conflict with the sovereigns continued until the peace of 1450 when the town alliance was broken up. In the same year, there were riots by the Rothenburg craftsmen who were demanding more rights of contribution. In 1455 they acquired the right to be elected to town council. Furthermore, the Jews who had settled numerously in the economically healthy town were banished from Rothenburg in 1350 and again in 1520, and their synagogue was destroyed. They had inhabited their own district around the White Tower.

The Era of the Reformation

Like in many other towns in Rothenburg the Lutheran ideas became accepted. The town joined the followers of Florian Geyer. Iconoclast Dr. Karlstadt incited millers to loot the Kobolzeller Chapel on Easter Monday in 1525. The art treasures were destroyed and the remains thrown into the river. In the same year, the peasant army was shattered by the Swabian alliance. On June 30th 1525 Markgraf Casimir von Ansbach ordered

a terrible punishment in Rothenburg whereby seventeen rebels were publically beheaded on the marketplace. In addition, every house in Rothenburg had to pay a penalty of seven guldens which for the poor families was especially difficult. Eventually the council decided to follow the Catholic religion again, but the people were cautious of the ideas particularly since the Deutschherren had become very careless in holding the service. In 1544 they engaged a protestant priest, but not until 1554 did the main church finally become protestant. In 1553 the wild Markgraf Albrecht von Brandenburg Kulmbach forced Rothenburg by many threats to join the Schmalkaldener alliance. One year later Albrecht was conquered, Rothenburg surrendered and was forced to pay 80,000 guldens as a war indemnity. The town would never again recover from this bleeding.

With Leonhard Weidmann, the town gained an excellent Renaissance architect. He built the Spital Bastei (the former hospital bastion), the characteristic Hegereiter House in the middle of the Spitalhof (hospital courtyard), the high school, and the artistic Baumeisterhaus (masterbuilder's house). One can admire the original form of the double house on a painting of St. Jacob's high altar. The eastern section burned in 1501, and not until 1572 was the foundation for the reconstruction laid. During this time, the fear of a water or bread shortage resulted in the construction of many fountains and the Ross Mill which allowed corn to be ground in the centre of town.

The Thirty Years War

The protestant sovereigns and towns along with Rothenburg allied with the union in 1608. In the year 1618 when the war began, the union held a meeting in Rothenburg. During the following years, Rothenburg did not only have to pay 25,000 guldens to the union, but in addition had to provide winter quarters to the allies as well as to the enemies who passed. Looters and wild hordes caused heavy damages in the surrounding villages, but until the fatal year 1631 the town was left untouched by the war activities.

Gustav-Adolf of Sweden had gained ground until Rothenburg and there took-up quarters. Upon departure, he left a small garrison to protect the town against imperial troops. Unfortunately, the imperial general Tilly had chosen Rothenburg as his winter quarter and demanded entrance. Because of their loyalty to their Swedish allies, the council denied and the ramparts were occupied. The predominance of the enemy did not permit a lengthy resistance especially after the powder reserve on the Klingen Bastion was exploded. After two days, the gate was opened. The imperial army had lost three hundred men, and in anger looted the town. At this point, the legend with the famous Meistertrunk (gigant gauge) began, and still surrounds this war day October 31st 1631. General Tilly angered with the vehement resistance was determined to execute four of the town councillors. All pleading was useless and Bürgermeister Bezold had to call upon the hangman. Meanwhile to soothe his mood, the best Franconian wine was offered to the general in a huge bumper which held 3¼ litres (about .86 gallons). In his temper, Tilly promised the town protection from looting and destruction if one of the town councillors emptied the bumper in one gulp. The former Bürgermeister Nusch accepted the challenge, and through his successful completion of the task, saved the town. However, the departing troops took supplies and weapons with them such that Rothenburg was unable to resist other bypassing troops. In 1632 Gustav-Adolf once more took his winter quarter here. The town again in 1634 was besieged and occupied by the imperial troops and forced to pay 30,000 guldens. Finally, in the year 1645 there was a successful siege of the French under Turenne. Two years after the end of the war in 1650 the last soldiers left the formerly rich town. To pay the 50,000 guldens the town was burdened with dept, and at the conclusion of war the exhausted town state for the first time had to obtain a loan. The number of inhabitants had shrunk by one-half due to war and pests. Rothenburg never recovered from that bleeding and the town sunk down to political insignificance. By 1802 Rothenburg had lost its imperial independence and became attached to Bavaria. This absolute stand-still in the town's development can be attributed to the severe pressures of the Thirty Years War. In turn what remained was the unfalsified impression of the Middle Age Rothenburg which became accessible to nineteenth century tourists. An air attack on Good Friday during World War II caused heavy damages. More than 300 houses, 6 official buildings, 9 towers, and 1 kilometer (about ⅔ miles) of the rampart were victimized. However, the panorama of the town was furtunately preserved since the architects had kept old plans. In this way Rothenburg again became a target for local and foreign tourists who come in increasing numbers every year to admire this jewel of the Middle Ages and allow their thoughts to flow into past times.

View over the marketplace: On the left the Meat and Dance Hall with the Herterichs Fountain, in the middle the Jagstheimer House and on the right the Town Hall.

At the Marketplace

Today as in the past the huge marketplace forms the lively centre of the town. It is dominated by an imposing Renaissance facade on one side while on the remaining three sides stand stately patrician houses. Here the locals congregate for their weekly marketing, and the tourists meet to begin their town tours. In addition, historical enactments and dances take place at this site. On the hour between 11.00 a.m. and 3.00 p.m., tourists assemble under the gable of the Ratsherrntrinkstube (the city's councillor's tavern), and await the opening of the Bull's-eye-windows. The two historical characters, General Tilly and former Bürgermeister Nusch, appear and celebrate the legendary Meistertrunk (giant gauge). The Town-Hall is considered one of the most impressive masterworks of German architecture. The side of the double building that faces away from the merketplace has a slender 60 m (197 ft) tower originating from the Gothic era (14th century). The similar front section was victimized by fire in 1501, and later replaced by the Rothenburg stone-mason and architect, Leonhard Weidmann, with a Renaissance structure facing the marketplace. He masterly connected the two sections in a harmonious manner. The strong horizontal lines of the German Renaissance were softened by the high bay window and the staircase tower. With its wide stairs, the façade of the Baroque arcades connects the imposing building to the uneven level of the marketplace. In the inner courtyard between the two buildings stands a picturesque Renaissance portal which is also one of Weidmann's masterpieces and was used as a temporary entrance for the new building before it was complete. Beneath in the cellar is located the dungeon containing a torture chamber and three narrow dark cells. In one of these cells, Rothenburg's most famous politician and general, Bürgermeister Toppler, died on June 13th 1408. The Gothic Kaisersaal (emperor's hall) contains a mighty woodframe ceiling and an artistic stone interior on the first floor.

Another Weidmann masterpiece can be found on the southeast corner of the marketplace. The Renaissance facade of the Masterbuilder's House is decorated with figures, and framed by gables of the older neighbouring houses. These male and female figures below the upper windows represent the seven virtues and seven vices.

On the southeast corner of the market, the framework gables of the imperial city's former Meat and Dance Hall and the Jagstheimer House form a picturesque background for Rothenburg's most attractive Renaissance fountain, the Herterichs Fountain (1608). The pillar in the centre exhibiting the statue of St. George on top is decorated with various coats of arms. The Jagstheimer House with its stylish bay window is considered to be one of the finest patrician houses of the town, and in 1513 was inhabited by Emperor Maximilian I.

Twilight: The picturesque Herterichs Fountain ▷ (1608), the Jagstheimer House (1488) and the Gothic Town-Hall (13th century) behind it.

◁ Town-Hall: Towards the market the Renaissance building with Baroque arcades, behind it the Gothic section with the high Town-Hall Tower. On the right The Ratsherrentrinkstube (Councillors' Tavern).

The Market Place with evening illumination. Between the Town-Hall and the Ratsherrentrinkstube (Councillors' Tavern) the tower helmets of St. Jacob's.

Picturesque Renaissance portal in the inner courtyard between the two parts of the Town-Hall,
main entrance in the 16th century.

◁ Court barriers made of stone in the Gothic Emperor's Hall of the Tower Hall.

◁ Soldiers play a game of dice. Exhibition Hall in the old Town-Hall. Stone barriers of a court in the Gothic Kaisersaal of the Town-Hall.

The Masterbuilder's House (1596): a Renaissance ▷ building by Weidmann, with Bürgermeister Toppler's House (17th century) on its right. The figures framing the windows represent the seven virtues and the seven vices.

The Masterbuilder's House: romantic inner court- ▷▷ yard with arcades and galleries.

The gable of the Ratsherrentrinkstube (Councillors' Tavern): Showing the Giant Gauge scene and the Capital's Clock, a Calendar Clock, the imperial eagle and a sun clock between the figures.

◁ A roofed draw well in Hofbronnen Lane near
the Herterichs Fountain.

Wrought iron emblem of the restaurant Eisenhut
(Iron Helmet). On the left the Town-Hall Tower
(195 feet high).

In the Herrngasse

The Herrngasse connects the marketplace with the site of the former castle. It is the widest street within the town walls. In former times, the horse and cattle market, a privilege of the masters and patricians, took place here. Today stately houses still frame the Herrnmarket and the original name has been maintained. Not one gable is like another. Above the attic windows there are great projecting beams, formerly used for hoisting loads of merchandise. In case of emergency and war, every household was required to store a specified quantity of foodstuffs and other essentials. Some of the honourable houses have preserved their romantic inner courtyards (numbers 11, 13, and 18). The Herrnfountain situated in the middle of the lane was built in 1595. The construction of fountains along with the necessary outside supply pipes was considered a major task by the town since their situation above the Tauber valley prevented the digging of deep wells. The conduits which brought water from outside of the walls were known only to the Bürgermeister and the town councillors. This secret was necessary to make it impossible for an enemy to cut off or poison the water supply.

The façade of the Staudtsche House (number 18) was decorated in 1772 with artistic wrought window gratings in the Rococo style. After destruction by fire, the building was replaced in 1678. The charming inner courtyard of the later house provides various forms through the columns, galleries, oriel window, and staircase tower. Before the fire, the stately house accomodated the Emperors Karl V and Ferdinand I as well as the wife of Gustav-Adolf, the Swedish Queen Eleonor. Across from the Staudtsche House stands the early Gothic Franciscan Church with its graceful side tower. It belonged to the beggar order of Franciscans who settled at Rothenburg in 1281. The church was inaugurated in 1309. A wooden barrier called the Lettner richly displays paintings, and is along with the church orchestral gallery especially remarkable. The Lettner operated as an additional division between the monks in the church gallery and the uninitiated congregation in the nave. This nave originates from the fourteenth century when the church was built. On the floore and walls, are found numerous particularly artistic gravestones and bronze plates representing Rothenburg's patrician families and aristocrates from the neighbouring country.

A statue on top of the main altar reveals the stigmatization of the holy Francis of Assisi, and exemplifies the late Gothic art work from 1400.

Herrngasse (Herrn Lane): proud patrician houses border Rothenburg's widest lane where formerly the horse market was held. In the foreground the Herrn Fountain (1595).

A picturesque fountain in the inner courtyard of the Hornberg House.

◁ The Herrn Fountain and the early Gothic Franciscan Church (1309). In the background the Burgtor (Castle Gate).

Franciscan Church: grave of the officer Hans von Beulendorf (†1504) and his wife Margarethe (†1496).

◁ Franciscan Church: the top of the altar and pictures on the wooden balustrade of the church gallery from the 14th century.

View from the Burgtor (Castle Gate) onto the Herrn Lane. The Town-Hall Tower and the mighty St. Jacob's Church elevate over the red brick roofs of the houses.

In the Burggarten (Castle Gardens)

The distant projection from the mountain marks the origin of the town. Protected by steep slopes on three sides, the first castle stood there even before the year 1000. After the Dukes of Rothenburg died out, the Hohenstaufens gained the inheritance, and erected in the rear section a second castle called the Vorderburg (front castle).

Both castles were destroyed by earthquake in 1356. The ruins became the property of the town now obligated to rebuild the chapel of the Vorderburg. In the year 1400, the chapel was consecrated in the honour of the holy Blasius, Sebastian, and Fabian, and has since been called Blasiuskapelle as well as "das Hohe Haus der Herzöge" (the honourable house of the dukes). In our century, this romantic building of the Staufers became a memorial to the dead, and the old wall murals were revealed. The other remains of the ruins were used for military construction and civilian dwellings in the town. In 1804, an administrative official did not realize the inestimable value of these already historical buildings and ordered the destruction of the crude Pharamund's Tower. It had been a part of the old earl's castle and was the only surviving structure after the earthquake.

The area of the Castle Gardens is today a well cultivated park site. From the natural terrace, a visitor has a charming view of the western military outline and over the Tauber Valley. Towards the town, the mighty gate forms both a border and a connection to the castle. This Tower Gate, the oldest and highest of Rothenburg, was erected in the 12th century. Slightly above and between the town's coat of arms, the imperial eagle, a symbol of the independent imperial town, can be recognized. The middle gate was originally bordered by battlements, but due to modern weapon techniques they became useless and were replaced by a hip roof. A draw bridge leads over an artificial moat into the Castle Gardens, and strengthened the defence of the castle gate. Finally in the 16th century, the richly decorated front gate with its two picturesque peak-roofed guard houses was added.

Burgtor (Castle Gate): highest and oldest gate ▷ tower of Rothenburg (12th century). The front gate with the guard houses built in the 16th century.

View from the Castle Gardens on the southern town fortification at the Kappenzipfel, with the remarkable Stöberleins Tower.

View from the castle gate towards the north. On the left the round prison tower and on the right the Klingen Gate.

The Klingen Bastion with St. Wolfgang's Church

At the end of the fourteenth century, the extended town wall was fortified in the north-west by the Klingen Gate, a massive tower 30 m (90 ft) high, fitted with four gracious bay windows. In the 16th century, a huge copper vat was installed to serve as the water supply for the numerous town fountains. The gate was further strengthened by a bastion that functions as a projected defence position. A gun platform on its west side protected the long northern section of the town wall. This north side is flanked by the fortified church, St. Wolfgang, and the additional outer gate strengthened by a draw bridge. Towards the wide moat, the church is equipped with loop-holes instead of the usual windows. Under the floor of the church rooms, casemates were built to confront enemies who may have proceeded across the moat. In the strong north wall of the fortified church, chapels were constructed along with a sacristy and a winding stairwell that lead to the casemates. Another staircase lead into the outer tower gate and to walkways elevated on the walls. At the end of the 15th century, this church was erected on the site of the shepherds' former place of prayer. St. Wolfgang was their patron saint who protected their herds against ravenous wolves. His picture can be seen in high relief between the portals and the outer walls under the crucifix. The attraction of the main altar is again St. Wolfgang flanked by the saints Sebastion and Rochus. The colourful woodcarvings possibly originate from the school of Tilman Riemenschneider. The paintings on the wings of the altar show scenes from the legends of the three saints. They, as well as the pictures on the Marien Altar, probably were painted by the Rothenburg artist, Wilhelm Ziegler.

The Dominican Nunnery

In 1250, Luitpold of Nortenberg donated his dairy farm to the Dominicans who in turn converted it into a monastery. It existed until the mid sixteenth century, and was inhabited by female members of the order, particularly unmarried aristocratic ladies. Today the buildings contain the Reichsstadtmuseums (imperial town museum) and the art gallery. The wood beamed ceilings of the oldest rooms were layed around 950 and the monastery kitchen itself is said to be the oldest in Germany. This kitchen along with several other characteristic rooms e.g. the Kräuterküche (spice kitchen) remain almost in their original condition. In additional rooms, valuable items from both the golden age of Rothenburg and the immediate past are displayed.

Klingen Gate: tower gate from the 14th century.
The upper floor with its elegant bay windows and ▷
bell tower later added.

The Mary Altar (around 1480) with the Madonna. ▷
The paintings on the wings resemble those of the main altar from Rothenburg artist W. Ziegler (around 1515).

St. Wolfgang's Church: on the shrine of the main ▷▷ altar from left to right the saints Sebastion, Wolfgang and Rochus.

Klingen Bastion: the roofed gun platform on the east side. From here it was possible to shot onto the area in front of the long north flank of the town rampart.

St. Wolfgang's Church (15th century): a forti- ▷ fication church with defence walkways and the north wall of the Klingen Bastion. On the left the outer gate tower is included.

The picturesque Feuerleins Bay Window in the ▷
Klingen Lane. In the background the St. Jacob's
Church with the archway under its western part.

The garden of the former Dominican Nunnery.
In the background the buildings of the Nunnery,
founded in 1265 and today is the Reichsstadt
Museum.

40

St. Jacob's Church

The mighty structure of Rothenburg's main church impressively dominates the town silhouette. Work was completed after more than one hundred years of construction in 1448, and the church provides an example of the high Gothic style. Typical for this architectural era are the fine open steeples of the twin towers and the numerous buttresses as well as the narrow high windows. The eyes of a visitor are purposely drawn upwards to God. An even stronger effect is achieved in the nave through its imposing height of 12 m (40 ft).

The long benches in the east choir were once reserved for members of the Deutschherren order, the builders of the church. At the end of the choir are found artistic medieval stained glass windows. However the main attraction of this section is the high altar called the Zwölfbotenaltar (altar of the twelve apostles) after the paintings on the lower predella. The sculpturing on the ornamented shrines show Mary, Jacob, Elizabeth, John, Leonard, and Antony at the feet of the crucified Christ. The pictures on the altar as well as the paintings on the predella originate from Friedrich Herlin (around 1430–1500) who worked mainly in Nördlingen. The inside of the wings reveal stages of Mary's life e.g. the annunciation, Christ's birth and circumcision, the visitation of the three wisemen, Christ in the temple, and Mary's death. On the outside, the legend of St. Jacob is shown. The first three pictures on the closed altar wings illustrate the capture and the execution of Jesus followed by the carriage of the body through the medieval town Rothenburg. The marketplace with the Gothic double town-hall before the catastrophic fire of 1501 is herein revealed, and provides one of the oldest and most interesting town pictures of this area.

St. Jacob's Church: Gothic church from around 1400 with differently formed twin towers, main church of Rothenburg.

◁ St. Jacob's Church: view through the nave towards the early Gothic east choir with the high
altar and the medieval windows.

Zwölfbotenaltar (Altar of the Twelve Apostles):
high altar of St. Jacob's Church. The wings and
predella with paintings from Friedrich Herlin
(15th century).

The Altar of the Twelve Apostles: the apostle Peter ▷
a figure from the painting on the predella.

The Altar of the Twelve Apostles: the painting
shows the Rothenburg Town-Hall before 1501.

46

The Holy Blood Altar,
a masterpiece of Tilman Riemenschneider

The western church gallery contains the most valuable item of St. Jacob's the Heiligblut-Altar (the holy blood altar). It is one of the most important works of wood-carver Tilman Riemenschneider (around 1460–1531). The richly decorated shrine exhibits the Last Supper masterpiece fully sculptured from linden wood. The traitor Judas is found in the middle of this unusual presentation. The bull's-eye window in the background enhances the projection effect of the masterpiece. The relief on the side wings shows Christ's procession to Jerusalem and the Mount of the Olives scene. Near the top of the altar, a golden cross elevates over Mary, an angel, and the crucifiction scene. This cross contains a case of rock crystal with a drop of Christ's blood in it, and gives the name, the Holy Blood Altar. To witness this precious relic was the goal of countless pilgrimages in the middle ages.

The Holy Blood Altar on the chair loft of St. Jakobs Church, a masterpiece of the famous carver Tilman Riemenschneider.

Part of the main group on the Holy Blood Altar's shrine (page 51).

The Holy Blood Altar: head of an apostle (page 52).

Resting apostle. Relief on the right wing of the Holy Blood Altar (page 53).

The Holy Blood Altar: scene of the Last Supper. Christ offers to Judas a piece of bread which gives evidence of Judas' betrayal.

The oldest Town Fortification and the Jewish District

After town rights were granted in the twelfth century the first rampart was erected. Similar to the wall of today it proceeded from the old castle and along the edge of the Tauber Valley, but then terminated at the Johannis Church of the former Dominican Nunnery. At the extension of the Judengasse (Jewish lane), the almost semi-circular street pattern following the old moat abviously marks the outline of the fortification. As well as this section containing the castle gate, only the Weisse Turm (white tower) and the Marcus Tower with the Röder Archway have been preserved since the town extension of 1204. The rampart itself was sold as construction material to citizens to build houses on the ground subsequently left useless by the formation of new defence lines.

A stately framework house, the Jewish Dancehall, was set close to the White Tower. This framework building was used for entertainment as well as a hostel for passing Jews. In its golden age, Rothenburg possessed a notable Jewish community of approximately 500 members. The midpoint of the community was the synagogue on the Marien Place which was surrounded by their residential district. In the thirteenth century, the famous and influential Rabbi Meir Ben Baruch (around 1215–1293) functioned. Around 1400, the Jewish community was moved to a new district, the Jewish Lane north of the White Tower up to the Schrannen Place. The old synagogue was changed into the Chapel Place, and hence invited the name Marien Place. Beside the Christian Cemetery, the Jewish graveyard was situated in the area of today's Schrannen Place. There the new synagogue also arose. In 1520, the Jewish community was completely banned from Rothenburg, and afterwards their synagogue was destroyed and their graveyard flattened. Only the dancehall with its attractive bay windows remained. This hall was used as a poor house called Seelhaus (soul house). In addition, the Renaissance fountain on the Marien Place is still called Seelbrunnen (soul fountain).

The mighty Marcus Tower originally was bordered with pinnacles whose shapes still can be seen by the interested observer below the steep hip-roof. The Büttelhaus (sheriff's house) next to the tower was used as a prison up intil the eighteenth century, and nowadays is occupied by Rothenburg's archives. Röder Archway, a former towngate, has a lanceolate roof. It is peculiar in that the gate and the extended roof are not positioned in the middle of the structure. This part of the Röder Lane with its picturesque framework houses, the simple Renaissance fountain, the Röder Archway at the end, and the Marcus Tower in the background belong to the most memorable impressions of the formally independent imperial town.

⊲ White Tower: part of the earliest town fortification
from the 12th century. On its left the Jewish Dance
Hall is included.

View from the Röder Tower onto the town. The houses between the Röder Gate and the White Tower on the right mark the outline of the oldest town fortification.

The Markus Tower and the Röder Archway which ▷
served as the town entrance from the east before
the first town extension.

Illumination of the Röder Gate at night, a romantic ▷▷
spot in the medieval town.

View from the Galgengasse (Gallows Lane) towards the White Tower. On the right the Jewish
Dance Hall with its neat bay window.

59

Along the Eastern Rampart

To the east towards the high plateau, the town fortification was always the most vulnerable. Both the northern Galgentor (the gallow's gate) and the Röder Gate had to be strengthened. During the Thirty Years War, Tilly (1631) and Turenne (1645) attacked this side of Rothenburg, and both marched into the town through the Gallow's Gate. In the middle ages, the gallows stood outside this gate, and consequently gave both the gate and the lane their names. During the first town extension in the thirteenth century, the gate was erected and later renewed in the following century after destruction by fire. After 1600, a moat was dug in front of the tower and the dungeon, and a drawbridge and mound positioned. As well as the Röder Gate, another massive bastion protected the town. From the Gallow's Gate, now also called the Würzburger Gate, there remains the inner tower gate and the front structure which once protected the drawbridge and dungeon. Almost simultaneous with the construction of the Gallow's Gate, the Röder Gate arose on the road to Ansbach. The dungeon was added in the fourteenth century while the bastion was added shortly before the beginning of the Thirty Years War. In order to reach the main gate, enemies had to overcome numerous barriers. The front gate was flanked by two guard houses and a stone bridge that could be destroyed in an emergency by the defenders. This bridge crossed the moat, and both could be reached by gunmen through loop-holes in the outer bastion gate and the rampart. If an enemy did manage to overcome the second gate, he would enter the main bastion, and then become trapped by a defence hallway enclosed at both ends. An additional part of the bridge which crossed the wide town moat was constructed as a drawbridge. In the drawn-up position, it protected the entrance into the front structure and the main gate in the rear. One easily imagines the considerable amount of funds collected from citizens in order to provide protection for towns during these troublesome times.

The mighty Faul Tower rises substantially above its neighbouring towers. Such a colossal tower was required to survey areas hidden from normal viewing. The saying goes that the tower is as deep as it is high. The lower section was at one time a starvation dungeon where prisoners putrefied.

The ramparts on the town's eastern side as well as several towers were heavily damaged at the end of the second world war. Soon after the war, these were rebuilt through donations, and the rampart was made walkable for two kilometers. The view over the roofs of neighbouring houses reveals the lack of building sites in the once rapidly expanding medieval town.

The Gallows Gate with the front structures. The ▷ eastern gate of the currently remaining fortification wall, construction has continued since 1204.

Röder Gate: in the background the Röder Tower (13th century) with the framework structure on top. The bastion was built in the 16th century to strengthen the tower.

Röder Bastion: the middle gate house with roofed defence walkways. In the background the arch of the front gate with the guard houses.

The Old Forge: romantic framework gable near the town wall. In the background the Röder Tower.

A part of the town wall. The narrow houses under the roofed defence walkway demonstrate the confinement inside the town fortification during the middle ages.

In the Spitalviertel (the former Hospital District)

The former Hospital of the Holy Ghost was built after 1280 outside the currently extended town fortification. In the fourteenth century, the so-called Kappenzipfel became enclosed by the wall. The hospital was built through a donation, and continued to grow through other numerous grants. It provided care for the sick and poor, and was also used as a hostel for travellers who came upon the town after sunset. The church at the northeast corner of the current structure is the sole remainder of the original complex. Many of the grave memorials and sculptures from the fourteenth and fifteenth centuries have been preserved, and offer a worthwhile viewing experience to the visitor. The lovely Hegereiter House forms an interesting contrast to the simplicity and practicality of the surrounding buildings. Its pointed roof and slim round stair tower with a delicate onion shaped dome is a jewel among the architectural relics of Rothenburg. The Hegereiter House as well as the unadorned main building was designed by the architect Leonard Weidmann. The hospital kitchen used to be on the first floor. The upper floor was temporarily occupied by the riding masters of the numerous hospital possessions. The main building with the gable side towards the road was first used for administration, and then later until 1948 as a hospital. Behind the beautiful wrought iron gate of the former baking house, a well installation is hidden. Next to it on the left stands the Pesthaus (the plague infirmary) with its isolation rooms. The massive barn that stored agricultural contributions stands on the western section of the hospital and belonged to the economic wing. It was constructed in 1699, and in honour of the 1975 European Year of the Protection of Monuments extended as a community centre called the Reichsstadt-Halle.

The southern town gate at the end of the Spital Lane is Rothenburg's most modern example. In front of the still elderly tower gate, a strong twin bastion in the shape of an octagon was placed. Leonard Weidmann was again the architect, and completed this structure in the sixteenth century. This town gate formed the mighty stronghold of Rothenburg along with the seven other gates protected by trap doors, a draw bridge, and the town rampart. The inscription "Pax intrantibus, salus exeuntibus" (Peace to the one who enters, sanity to the one who leaves) is found on the outer gate arch, and contrasts with the formidable air of the tower.

Another important military structure in the Spital district was the Rossmühle (the horse mill). In case of flour delivery cancellation from the numerous mills in the Tauber Valley because of war or drought, this mill site became necessary. Sixteen horses walking in a circle moved the four sets of millstones. This massive building with its strong buttresses is used today as a youth hostel.

Spital District (the Old Hospital District) with the tower gate and bastion. Between the widely spread buildings of the former hospital stands the decorative Hegereiter House.

View on the south of St. Jacob's and the Town- ▷
Hall tower. On the right the roof and tower of the
Johannis Church.

Spital Gate: view through the front gate onto the
entrance of the bastion (16th century) which is
the mightiest defence structure of the town fortification.

Siebers Tower: this was the southern town gate ▷
until it lost importance when the Spital district
was fortified in the 14th century.

The Hegereiter House: in the Spital yard built in
1591 by L. Weidmann. On the ground floor is the
Spital kitchen.

At the Plönlein

The Plönlein is one of the most typical sites of Rothenburg, and offers a simultaneous view of two towers. In the beginning, the name was probably "Plänlein" derived from the Latin word "planum" meaning even place. It is just a fork in the Unteren Schmied-gasse (the lower smith lane) shortly before the Siebers Tower. The slope climbing from the Tauber Valley reaches the town at the Kobolzeller Gate, and then at the Unteren Schmiedgasse connects with the level streets. The wrought iron insignia hang on several ornate houses to announce a restaurant or a workshop. A delicate framework gable separates the two lanes. The picturesque column fountain in front of this gable reveals the year inscription 1667. Both tower gates arose with the first town extension at the beginning of the thirteenth century, and between them one can still see the re-mains of a connecting wall. After the Spital district was enclosed during the fourteenth century by the town's fortification, the Siebers Tower lost its importance, but was maintained as an architectural memorial.

The Kobolzeller Gate forms the only entrance from the valley. During the town's second extension, a square bastion was built in front of the tower gate. Due to the steep inclination the outer gate was not supplied with a tower, but instead this structure was erected on the nearby mountain side. From this Kohl Tower, the rampart proceeded to the south. A covered walkway on top of the wall connected the towers. Over the pointed archway is found Rothenburg's decorative coat of arms, an eagle representing the imperial town and the towers. A small building protected by the outer doors was used by the gate patrolmen. The small platform surrounded by pinnacles is nicknamed the Devil's Pulpit. The Gothic Johannis Church marks the frontier to the oldest section of the town. When it was erected around 1400, some parts of the then useless rampart were enclosed in the structure. At its east wall, one can still see the frame of the former Johanniter Gate. In the main building of the holy complex is now situated the medieval crime museum. Shown in various sections, this unique collection covers such diversified areas as instruments of judgement, torture and punishment, decrees pertaining to medieval laws, medals, wax imprinted documents, seals, graphics, and caricatures. The museum offers a complete look into the laws and legal climate of the so-called good old times.

Plönlein: famous street bifurcation at the Schmied-gasse (Smith Lane) with a view of the Siebers Tower on the left and the Kobolzeller Gate.

Plönlein at night: the romantic illumination emphasizes the simple beauty of the framework gables and the mighty towers.

Kobolzeller Gate at the edge of the Tauber Valley. ▷
Entrance to the bastion with the town's code of
arms and the Kohl Tower on the right. In the
background the Siebers Tower.

Artistic forged emblem of the Hotel Zum Hirschen.

Medieval Crime Museum: instruments of punishment. On the upper left the "Schandmantel" for alcoholics. On the right the "Iron Virgin". Below an interrogation chair, a stretching bench, and an interrogation table with a thumb screw.

Section of the Burggasse (Castle Lane) with the patrician house "Zur Höll" (to Hell), the oldest dwelling of Rothenburg.

Aerial view of Rothenburg: medieval development of the town is clearly outlined. The rampart towards the high plateau remains complete.

On the Taubergrund (Bottom of the Tauber Valley)

Below the Spital district the river is crossed by an unusual looking double bridge. It is constructed from two layers of viaducts, and resembles the aqueducts of the Roman era. Probably the structure was initially erected in 1330, but later on the side which faces the river the piers were further strengthened. However Merian engraving from 1648 does portray the bridge with a slightly different shape. The traffic lanes run across the lower viaduct while the upper arch is endowed only with side walls. In 1732 the bridge was destroyed by a flood, but was rebuilt in the following years. We can assume that at this time the bridge acquired its present form.

On the east river bank near the double bridge the Kobolzeller Chapel stands with its neat ridge turret tower. The late Gothic church was used in the nineteenth century as a dye house as well as a barn, and was nearly torn down. It was then bought by King Max II of Bavaria who restored and donated the structure to the Catholic community. The chapel contains only one nave, but does possess a richly decorated reticular ceiling, a fine parapet, and a remarkable winding staircase made of two lanes that provide two ways to climb or descend the stairs. The chapel's former rich furnishings were victimized by the image-breaker Dr. Karlstadt who lived in Rothenburg for a long time. A couple of mill workers were incited by Karlstadt, and subsequently entered the chapel on Easter Monday in 1525, destroyed the art objects, and flung their remains into the river.

Numerous mills took advantage of the energy provided by the Tauber current. One example is the Herren Mill located across the river from the Kobolzeller Chapel. Below the Castle Gardens the unique Toppler Castle elevates from the bottom of the valley. It was constructed in 1388 by the Bürgermeister Toppler as a water castle, and had been modelled after the romantic towers of the aristocrats. Here Toppler allegedly conserved with King Wenzel on several occasions. The castle is decorated with the coat of arms, and is almost completely furnished in the original style of its builder.

The village of Detwang is situated slightly further down the river. The Romanic parish church built around 1150 is older than the one in Rothenburg, and later its inside was restored in the Gothic style. The head pieces of the altar were finished around 1500. The sculptured grouping in the shrine of the main altar presents one of Tilman Riemenschneider's masterpieces. Originally he had created the grouping around 1510 for Rothenburg's Michaelis Chapel which was heavily damaged during the Thirty Years War and torn down soon after. The altar was subsequently brought to Detwang, and probably around this time provided with the contemporary simple shrine. We can see the mourning group with Mary and John on the left side of the crucifix, and on its right the lieutenant, his soldiers, and the high priest. This figure grouping was hand carved by Riemenschneider himself while the reliefs of the Mount Olives scene and Christ's resurrection on the altar wings were made by his assistants.

View over the romantic double bridge in the bottom of the Tauber Valley with the silhouette of the medieval town above.

Toppler Castle: built in the 14th century for ▷
Bürgermeister Toppler. A water castle modelled
after the romantic aristocratic towers.

Rothenburg on the plateau over the Tauber Valley.
On the left the tower-like Toppler Castle.

Subtitles of pages 88 and 89.

Sitting room of the famous Bürgermeister Toppler.
Here he met several times with King Wenzel for
political talks.

Toppler Castle: kitchen with fire place and furniture
from the 14th century.

Detwang: a romantic village in the Tauber Valley
below Rothenburg. Romanic Parish Church (12th
century) with the Riemenschneider Altar.

Crucifix Altar in the Parish Church of Detwang.
The main part is attributed to Riemenschneider.
On the left the group with Mary and on the right
soldiers and a priest.

The Historical Festival "Der Meistertrunk" (the Giant Gauge)

Once a year at Whitsuntide the historical event is enacted in Rothenburg by the local actors. The play was premiered in 1881, and portrays the remarkable rescue of the town on October 31, 1631 during the Thirty Years War. The legend says that Tilly the imperial general of the Catholic allies appears with some of his troops at the town wall, and requests entrance and winter quarter. The protestant town is currently occupied by Swedish troops, and presumably to respect this alliance the councillors refuse entrance to Tilly. Hence a battle begins. Furthermore the town anticipates help from Gustav-Adolf after receiving announcement that a large regiment is approaching. However these troops are actually additional aid for the imperial enemy. In the beginning the battle is equally balanced, but later on Rothenburg's gun powder reserves explode and the Klingen Bastion is consequently destroyed. In turn the town surrenders and Tilly finally enters. Angered by the unexpected and strong resistance he threatens to loot and destroy the town, and as well demands execution of the four councillors. No entreaties can change his mind, and Bürgermeister Bezold is sent to call the hangman. Meanwhile the general is offered the best Franconian wine in an attempt to soothe his temper. The mighty bumper that holds 3¼ l (.86 gallons) is also handed over to his officers. Tilly's mood does improve, and he promises mercy to the town and its councillors if one of them can empty the bumper in one draught. After an initial hesitation the former Bürgermeister Nusch decides to accept the challenge. He succeeds and Tilly keeps his promise. Hence the town is saved, and the townspeople shout with joy.

In addition to the presentation of this play in the Kaisersaal of the town-hall, Rothenburg offers to its visitors a historical program of wide variety e.g. the Hans Sachs plays. During the main season, a Rothenburg theatre group presents the farces of the famous shoemaker poet Hans Sachs several times. The costumes of both the actors and the musical accompaniment shift the spectators back into the middle ages. On several Sundays of the year, a dance troupe meets at the Rathaus Place to perform the historical Shepherds' Dance. Traditionally the shepherds had danced around the Herterichs Fountain to demonstrate their joy for the end of the plague. The high-light of the festive session is the enactment of the entry of the imperial troops on the afternoon of Whit-Monday. Tilly's soldiers complete with historical costumes and weapons proceed from the Spital Gate into the town. The precession terminates at the Gallow's Gate where a colourful army camp is formed.

◁ Historical shepherds dance in the decorated Marketplace.

Historical Scene at the Herrn Fountain: bakers who sold underweight bread were thrown into the fountain as punishment for unscrupulous behaviour. ▷

The Meistertrunk (Giant Gauge) play in the Kaisersaal at the Town-Hall. Past Bürgermeister Nusch empties the bumper in one draught. On the left General Tilly with his men and on the right the town councillors.

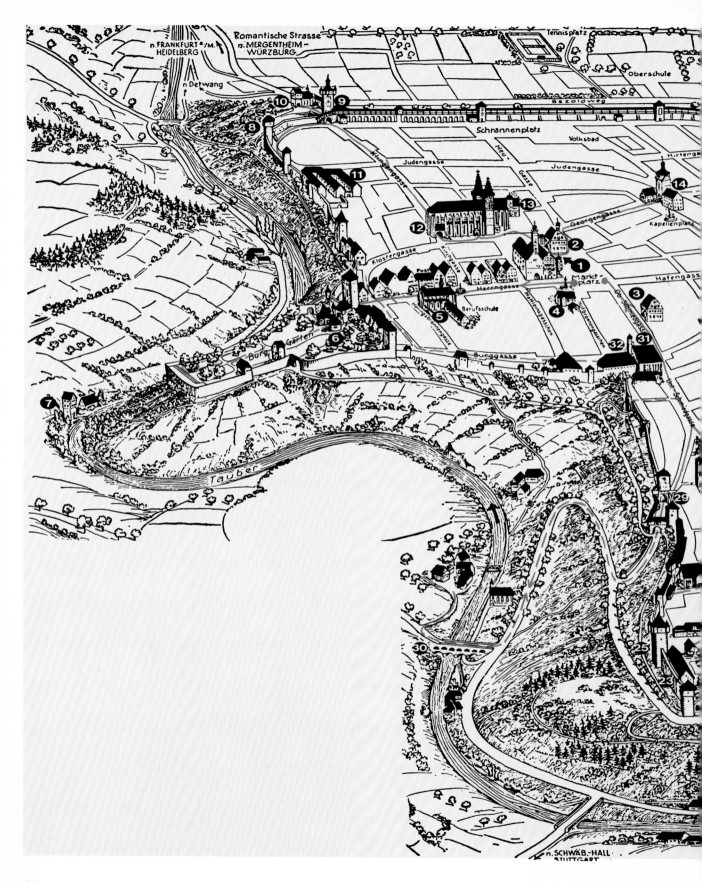

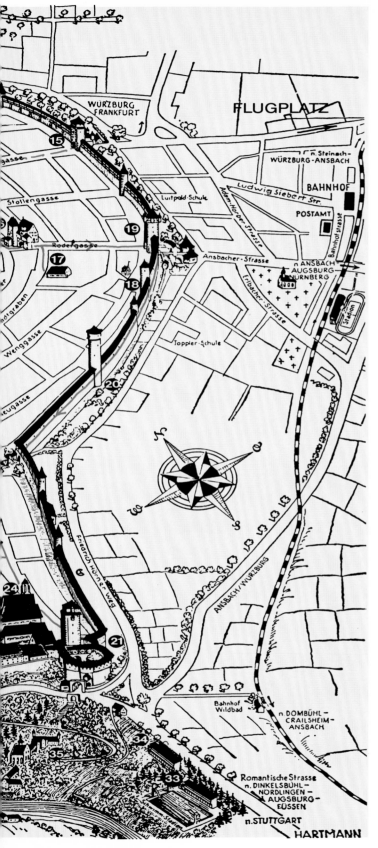

1 Rathaus
2 Ratstrinkstube
3 Baumeisterhaus
4 Fleisch- u. Tanzhaus
5 Franziskanerkirche
6 Burgtor
7 Topplerschlößchen
8 Strafturm
9 Klingentor
10 Wolfgangskirche
11 Reichsstadtmuseum
12 St.-Jakobs-Kirche
13 Ehem. Gymnasium
14 Weißer Turm
15 Galgentor
16 Markusturm
17 Alt-Rothenburger
   Handwerkerhaus
18 Alte Schmiede
19 Rödertor
20 Faulturm
21 Spitalbastei
22 Hegereiterhaus
23 Reichsstadthalle
24 Spitalkirche
25 Stöberleinsturm
26 Roßmühle
27 Siebersturm
28 Plönlein
29 Kobolzeller Tor
30 Doppelbrücke
31 Johanniskirche
32 Kriminalmuseum
33 Schwimmstadion
34 Hallenbad
35 Wildbad

Pictures of Rothenburg